ENVIRONMENTAL ISSUES

By Gemma McMullen

KidHaven
PUBLISHING

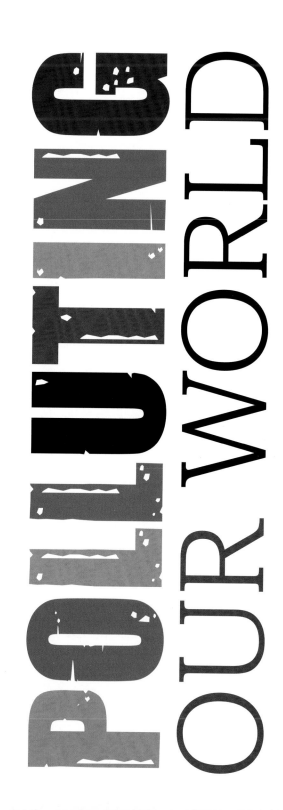

POLLUTING OUR WORLD

Published in 2017 by
KidHaven Publishing, an Imprint of Greenhaven Publishing, LLC
353 3rd Avenue
Suite 255
New York, NY 10010

Designer: Ian McMullen
Editor: Gemma McMullen

Cataloging-in-Publication Data

Names: McMullen, Gemma.
Title: Polluting our world / Gemma McMullen.
Description: New York : KidHaven Publishing, 2017. | Series: Environmental issues | Includes index.
Identifiers: ISBN 9781534520455 (pbk.) | ISBN 9781534520479 (library bound) | ISBN 9781534520462 (6 pack) | ISBN 9781534520486 (ebook)
Subjects: LCSH: Pollution–Environmental aspects–Juvenile literature. | Environmental protection–Juvenile literature.
Classification: LCC TD176.M36 2017 | DDC 363.73–dc23

Printed in the United States of America

CPSIA compliance information: Batch #CW17KL: For further information contact Greenhaven Publishing LLC, New York, New York at 1-844-317-7404.

Please visit our website, www.greenhavenpublishing.com. For a free color catalog of all our high-quality books, call toll free 1-844-317-7404 or fax 1-844-317-7405.

Words in **bold** can be found in the glossary on page 24.

Photo Credits: Abbreviations: l–left, r–right, b–bottom, t–top, c–center, m–middle.
All images are courtesy of Shutterstock.com.
Cover – Chris DeRidder. 1 – M. Shcherbyna. 2 – M. Shcherbyna. 3t – TranceDrumer. 3b – Nuttapong. 4 – TSpider. 5 – Alexander Tihonov. 6 – Hung Chung Chih. 7 – Balu. 8 – smikeymikey1. 9 – OPgrapher. 10 – Toa55. 11bg – BMJ. 11inset – cubephoto. 12bg – Mrs_ya. 12inset – fluke samed. 13 – Willyam Bradberry. 14 – kwest. 15 – Anna Omelchenko. 16l – 3445128471. 16r – Andrey_Popov. 17bg – Alan Tunnicliffe. 17inset – Alan Tunnicliffe. 18 – udra11. 19: tl – Ansis Klucis; tc – Kaspars Grinvalds; tr – Kaspars Grinvalds; b nito. 20 – Maciej Bledowski. 21 – David W. Leindecker. 22l – studioloco. 22r – avel L Photo and Video. 23bg – Monkey Business Images. 23inset – Pavel L Photo and Video.

CONTENTS

WHAT IS POLLUTION?

Pollution happens when something **contaminates** its natural surroundings. We call something that pollutes an area a pollutant. Pollutants are generally waste materials.

There are many different types of pollution, some of which we will explore in this book. Pollution causes negative changes to be made to the environment, which can affect our lives and the lives of the animals around us.

AIR POLLUTION

Air pollution is the most dangerous type of pollution because we breathe it in. Air pollution generally **occurs** when a fuel is burned and releases harmful chemicals into the air.

Smoke from chimneys, factories, vehicles, and fires are all air pollutants. When garbage is burned, the chemicals released into the air cause pollution. That's why it's important for us to reduce the amount of garbage we create by reusing and recycling.

Everyday activities such as driving and cooking cause air pollution.

ASTHMA

Asthma is a medical condition that affects the lungs and makes it hard for people to breathe. Air pollution is thought to increase difficulties for people with asthma, and it possibly even causes asthma.

PEOPLE WHO HAVE ASTHMA USE AN INHALER.

ACID RAIN

When the air is heavily polluted, the pollution can get into the rain that falls back down to Earth. Polluted rain is called acid rain.

Did you know that acid rain is dangerous for plants and animals and can cause them to die?

WATER POLLUTION

Water pollution is when our seas, rivers, and lakes are polluted. Water pollution can be caused by acid rain. It can also be caused by oil spills and **industrial** waste being dumped into rivers.

Water pollution has a huge impact on many **species** that live in or on the water. Many fish and animals become sick and die because of water pollution. Even people can be affected because we eat fish that may have been poisoned.

OIL SPILLS

Oil spills at sea are generally far more damaging than those on land because they can spread for hundreds of miles on the water. Oil spills on land are far easier to contain to one area.

BIRDS, FISH, MAMMALS, AND SHELLFISH CAN ALL BE KILLED BY OIL.

DIRTY WATER

Litter that finds its way into the sea is a type of water pollution. Litter can be harmful to sea creatures. Sea turtles can mistake plastic bags for jellyfish and eat them, which causes them to **suffocate.**

HEAT AND LIGHT POLLUTION

Heat pollution, or thermal pollution, creates an **excess** of heat in the environment. It increases the temperature of Earth and has been linked to **climate change**.

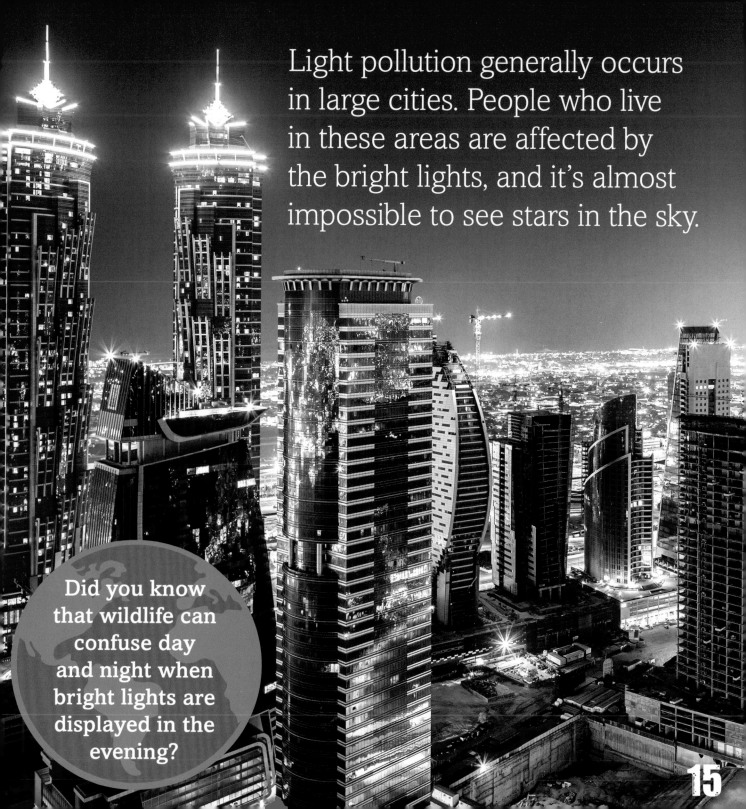

Light pollution generally occurs in large cities. People who live in these areas are affected by the bright lights, and it's almost impossible to see stars in the sky.

Did you know that wildlife can confuse day and night when bright lights are displayed in the evening?

NOISE POLLUTION

Noise pollution happens when too much noise has a negative effect on people or animals. Noise pollution is often caused by machines or vehicles. Unwanted noise can cause **sleep disturbances**, hearing problems, and high stress levels.

LOUD NOISES CAN CAUSE TROUBLE SLEEPING.

Noise pollution can also cause problems for wildlife. Too much noise can stop animals from communicating with each other, which makes it difficult to hunt or mate.

SOIL POLLUTION

Soil is extremely important because it's where plants grow. We need soil in order to live, but soil can become polluted, too.

WE NEED SOIL TO GROW PLANTS.

Soil mostly gets polluted by chemicals that people use for industry or farming. Sometimes, accidents can cause soil pollution, such as stored oil or chemical leaks.

Since much of the food we eat grows in soil, it's possible that people could be made sick by soil pollution. Plants aren't able to grow as well in soil that's not healthy.

SOIL POLLUTION

FAILED CROPS

HUMAN ILLNESS

LITTER

Litter is waste that's dropped onto the ground, rather than put into a can. Litter is a form of pollution because it can affect people, animals, and the ground below.

Litter is very unclean and can ruin the way a place looks. It can be dangerous to animals because they might eat or get trapped in the litter.

GARBAGE IS HARMFUL TO ANIMALS.

Even though it's bad for the environment, some people still choose to litter!

HOW CAN WE HELP?

There are a number of things that each of us can do to decrease the level of pollution in our world:

CHOOSE TO WALK OR RIDE A BIKE RATHER THAN TRAVELING IN A CAR.

ASK THE ADULTS YOU LIVE WITH TO ONLY USE NATURAL PRODUCTS AROUND THE HOME AND IN THE GARDEN.

NEVER DROP YOUR GARBAGE ON THE GROUND. IF YOU CAN'T FIND A CAN, THEN TAKE IT HOME.

TURN LIGHTS OFF WHEN YOU LEAVE A ROOM.

SPEND A DAY WITH AN ADULT AND SOME FRIENDS PICKING UP THE GARBAGE IN A LOCAL FIELD OR PARK.

23

GLOSSARY

climate change	a change in the weather or temperature of a large area
contaminates	makes something unclean by adding to it
excess	a large amount
industrial	referring to large factories where things are made
occurs	happens
sleep disturbances	not being able to sleep well
species	a kind or sort of living thing
suffocate	be unable to breathe

INDEX

24